Midnight Forests

A Story of Gifford Pinchot
and Our National Forests

by **Gary Hines**

Illustrated by **Robert Casilla**

Boyds Mills Press

The publisher wishes to thank Lori Danuff McKean, Information and Education Specialist, USDA Forest Service, Grey Towers National Historic Landmark, Milford, Pennsylvania, and the dedicated staff of Grey Towers, for reviewing the manuscript and providing the historic photo reference, which forms the basis for many of the book's illustrations.

Published by Boyds Mills Press, Inc.
A Highlights Company
815 Church Street
Honesdale, Pennsylvania 18431
Printed in China

Library of Congress Cataloging-in-Publication Data

Hines, Gary.
Midnight forests : a story of Gifford Pinchot and our national forests / by Gary Hines ; illustrated by Robert Casilla.— 1st ed.
p. cm.
Includes bibliographical references and index.
ISBN 1-56397-148-8 (alk. paper) 1. Pinchot, Gifford, 1865-1946—Juvenile literature. 2. Foresters—United States—Biography—Juvenile literature. 3. Conservationists—United States—Biography—Juvenile literature. [1. Pinchot, Gifford, 1865-1946. 2. Foresters. 3. Conservationists.] I. Casilla, Robert, ill. II. Title.

SD129.P5M53 2004 333.75'16'092—dc22

2003026876

First edition, 2005
The text of this book is set in 13-point Caxton Light.

Visit our Web site at www.boydsmillspress.com

10 9 8 7 6 5 4 3 2 1 hc

To the Frosters, especially Martha
—G. H.

For Agustin Torres, who had a great love of nature
—R. C.

LONG AGO, IN 1885, at his summer estate in Pennsylvania, James Pinchot planted an idea into his young son Gifford, who was just about to leave for college. "How would you like to be a forester?" the older Pinchot asked. James, who had made a fortune importing fine wallpapers, had seen forestry practiced in Europe. He was now concerned about the destruction of America's forests.

GIFFORD DIDN'T KNOW A THING about forestry, but he loved the woods. And so, as he began his studies at Yale University, the idea grew. But he found that no one there—or anywhere else in the United States—knew much about forestry. He took courses in biology and geology, but he learned very little about protecting and managing trees.

After Pinchot graduated from Yale, he was offered a job by his grandfather Amos Eno, a wealthy real estate investor in New York City. Eno thought forestry was a silly idea.

Pinchot turned down the job. "There are things higher than business," he wrote later. Instead, he boarded a ship and crossed the sea to Europe, intending only to buy a book or two about forestry during his European travels and return home. But in Germany he met a famous forestry professor, Dr. Dietrich Brandis, who suggested that Pinchot attend forestry school in France.

Pinchot spoke French about as well as he spoke English. His ancestors were French. As a boy, he had been tutored in the language and had traveled to France many times with his parents. He decided to take Dr. Brandis's advice.

AT L'ECOLE NATIONALE FORESTIERE, Pinchot learned that Europeans, who had once nearly destroyed their forests, had now developed ways to cut some trees and keep others growing. He learned how improper logging that removed all the trees left behind soil without any vegetation to hold it in place. When rains later washed the valuable soil away, nothing could grow in the logged area.

Pinchot also studied ways of preparing land for the planting of new trees, a forestry practice called silviculture. He learned how to survey land and make maps, and how wildlife depends on the forest for food and shelter.

After a year Pinchot came home, eager and full of big ideas about saving America's forests. He came back just in time. The population of the United States was growing by leaps and bounds. People needed huge amounts of wood for buildings, railroad ties, fuel, furniture, paper, and even pencils. To meet that need, lumber companies were quickly destroying the forests in many areas, cutting down every tree and leaving bare, ugly hillsides behind.

PINCHOT SPENT TIME IN THE WOODS whenever he could. He learned more about logging by talking with lumberjacks. "Awestruck and silent," he slept under the stars at the Grand Canyon. He rode his horse through the giant sequoias of California and ran like a boy under Yosemite Falls. He even traded stories with the great naturalist John Muir.

FINALLY, AS THE FIRST AMERICAN CITIZEN trained in forestry, Pinchot was ready to start giving out advice. Unfortunately, not many people wished to hear it. Wealthy lumbermen wanted to keep cutting trees as fast as possible, so they could make money as quickly as possible. Forest lovers wanted to save every tree and stop loggers from cutting entirely. Neither group wanted to compromise.

Pinchot believed that "trees could be cut and the forests preserved, at one and the same time." He was determined to show the country how this could be done.

A wealthy southerner named George Vanderbilt hired Pinchot to take care of the forest on his huge Biltmore Estate in North Carolina. Pinchot took notes, drew maps, and told the loggers there that they would have to change their ways. He said they could no longer cut all the trees and leave behind a big mess. Pinchot showed them how to thin out the small trees so they had more room to grow, and to make sure that bigger trees fell where they wouldn't hurt anything.

PINCHOT'S APPROACH WORKED. The grumbling loggers made money, and the forest remained healthy. When people began to notice Pinchot's success, they invited him to make speeches. Punching the air with his fist, he said that if trees were cut properly, soil erosion could be controlled and society's demand for wood could be met without destroying the forests.

In 1898, Secretary of Agriculture James Wilson appointed Pinchot to lead the federal government's tiny forestry department in Washington, D.C. At the time, the department merely gave out information. The forests were actually controlled by the Land Department. Pinchot wanted forests and foresters together in the Department of Agriculture, with himself in charge.

IN WASHINGTON, HE MET POWERFUL PEOPLE. One, the governor of New York, invited him to a friendly boxing match. Pinchot promptly flattened the stout governor with a roundhouse to the chin. The two men became good friends, and the governor, Theodore Roosevelt, was soon elected Vice President of the United States. When an assassin shot President William McKinley in 1901, Roosevelt became the president.

Pinchot and Roosevelt had much in common. Both knew a lot about the West, loved the outdoors, and liked to hunt and fish. They worked hard and played hard. With Pinchot in tow, the new president delighted in hiding from his bodyguards. They also swam together in the Potomac River, sometimes taking important and dignified people along with them. Once, when Pinchot returned soaking wet to his parents' home in Washington, D.C., the maid scolded him. "You've been out with that president!" she accused.

IN 1905, WITH ROOSEVELT'S HELP, Pinchot managed to get all federal forests put under his control. He quickly reorganized his department and renamed it the Forest Service, saying it had to serve "the greatest good of the greatest number in the long run."

Next, he hired more forest rangers. He wanted the rangers to be strong, like hard work, and know a lot about trees and animals. Pinchot thought the rangers should have outdoor experience, even if they were not well educated, men who could also "make simple maps and write intelligent reports."

Pinchot told his rangers to serve the public, fight fires, and see that the forests were properly used. He said if visitors make mistakes, they should be shown the right way to do things rather than being punished. He directed his rangers to be polite.

SOON PINCHOT AND PRESIDENT ROOSEVELT found themselves in a great race. To encourage settlement of the West and raise money for the government, Congress had for several years been selling land to settlers as quickly as it could. Lumber, water, and mining companies wanted some of that land, too, and had often used illegal means to obtain it. They convinced individuals to buy parcels of land and then turn the deeds over to the companies. These companies began to accumulate large tracts of land rich in natural resources, which was not the intent of Congress. Pinchot called these companies "land thieves." He and President Roosevelt wanted the best forests protected from waste and destruction.

Pinchot hired top horseback riders to run surveys and make maps showing which areas contained outstanding forests. Then President Roosevelt, using power given to him by the Forest Reserve Act of 1891, protected those lands by designating them national forests. Their actions angered some people—especially congressmen in the West, whose districts included big companies that wanted the land for themselves.

In response, Pinchot explained that setting aside forests did not prevent lumber companies from cutting trees. The companies just had to be more careful and leave some trees standing to help conserve the forests. Mining companies could still mine, hunters could still hunt, and anglers could still fish—as long as they followed the rules, obeyed Pinchot's rangers, and in some cases paid a fee.

Nevertheless, the fight went on. Those who didn't want forests protected lobbied for a law that would prevent Roosevelt from setting aside any more forest land. When the time came for Congress to vote on it in 1907, the law passed. There were still many forested areas that Pinchot and the president wanted to protect. Roosevelt felt he could not veto the new law because it was part of an agricultural bill that was important to the nation's farmers. It appeared that they would be handcuffed by the Congress.

But Pinchot had an idea. As he proposed his idea to the president, a big grin spread across Roosevelt's face. Within hours, the two men were poring over big, unrolled maps. Ten days remained until the president had to sign the bill into law. Until then, he could keep setting new lands aside as national forests.

PINCHOT RETURNED TO HIS OFFICE. "Now we get busy," he told his staff. They began working secretly around the clock, burning the midnight oil. Telegrams flashed back and forth to and from rangers in the West. Pinchot and his staff studied maps, read reports, and hastily drew up new forest boundaries. Stenographers and secretaries dropped everything and typed papers for the president to sign. Pinchot met often with Roosevelt.

When the day for Roosevelt's signature arrived, he and Pinchot were on their hands and knees in the White House study, feverishly checking over maps and papers spread before them. Roosevelt fired off one question after another. "Have you put in the Flathead?" he asked. Pinchot nodded. "Bully! Up there one winter I saw the biggest yard of black-tailed deer!"

FINALLY, ROOSEVELT SMILED and stood up. He dusted off his knees and swept papers from his desk. Dipping his stub pen in the inkwell, he grinned broadly. "Bring 'em on," he said. Pinchot handed him a stack of proclamations. By signing them, Roosevelt turned 16 million additional acres of western lands into new national forests. Only then did he sign the new law passed by Congress.

Pinchot and Roosevelt knew their opponents would be furious when they found out they'd been hoodwinked. But the president and the forester were delighted. The signed proclamations ensured that these national forests would be protected and managed for the future use of all people, not given to those who were motivated solely by profit.

PRESIDENT ROOSEVELT'S TERM IN OFFICE ended on March 4, 1909. The new president, William H. Taft, did not agree with Pinchot's conservation ideas. On February 7, 1910, Taft fired Pinchot from his job as chief forester. But the firing created such a public stir that Taft softened his views and soon gave the conservation movement more support.

Gifford Pinchot's U.S. Forest Service still exists today, as an agency within the Department of Agriculture that employs more than thirty thousand people. The 16 million acres of forest lands that Pinchot and Roosevelt gave to the American people on March 2, 1907, remain known as "the Midnight Forests," and Gifford Pinchot is remembered as America's first and most influential forester.

AFTERWORD

Eventually, most people wound up accepting forestry, a science that Gifford Pinchot later included in a broader idea called conservation. Although Pinchot did not invent this word, he was the first to define conservation as the wise use and scientific management of all the country's natural resources.

Many of the issues of Pinchot's day are still being contested. Some individuals and companies want the national forests removed from government protection; others want the forests left in an entirely natural, undisturbed state. People on both extremes often consider the Forest Service an obstacle to their desires.

Most Americans, however, fall somewhere in between. Millions are glad that the Midnight Forests remain protected national treasures for everyone to enjoy.

Sources

McGeary, Nelson M. *Gifford Pinchot: Forester Politician*. Princeton, N.J.: Princeton University Press,1960.

Steen, Harold K. *The U.S. Forest Service: A History*. Seattle: University of Washington Press, 1976.

Greeley, William B. *Forests and Men*. Garden City, N.Y.: Doubleday & Company, Inc., 1956.

Gifford Pinchot, *Breaking New Ground*. Covelo, Ca. Island Press, reprinted 1998 (originally published 1947).